A Guide to Cyber Safety, Internet Security and Protection

for Kids, Teens, Parents and Professionals

DR. SCOTT MITNICK

DEDICATION

To All
Cyber Security Experts
And Internet Safety Gurus
who protect our cyberworld

CONTENTS

1 INTERNET SAFETY AND CYBER SECURITY

- **Mary buys her wares** and goods regularly from a particular online shop and enjoyed their services. Her address, credit card details were stored on this shop's database or server for easy and quicker transaction. Then one day she received an email assumed to have come from the online shop, claiming she'd qualified for a discount. Who wouldn't be happy? She filled in the qualification forms or discount coupons with the required details - credit card, SSN, etc. She thought it was the normal verification details demanded at each transaction. Not long some substantial amount of money was withdrawn from her bank account. The online shop noticed suspicious user from a third party. The email to Mary was fake. This type of attack is called cyber-attack and the attacker is called a hacker. The hacker used the form she filled to get her credit card details and carried out the fraudulent activity. A cyber security setup or proper internet security practices would have protected her device and account if she had one or was aware of these attacks. With chip connectivity these days of housewares, from refrigerators to spoon to doorbells and even to dog plate etc. IOTs (Initialism of Internet of things), a self-configuring wireless network between objects expose us to insecurities.

- Internet safety, e-safety or cyber safety is the act of protecting yourself, your accounts and devices from cybercrimes and attacks online. Just as we need physical locks, keys, security officers and police to minimize crime in the physical world so we need them in the virtual world to mitigate crime. You must be aware of the risks involved with online activities and employ a few strategies to prevent or avoid these risks. This can help you, your kids and family from being exposed to the risk of selling out vital family information to cyber criminals or materials that could harm your devices. It's smart to teach children computer safety so that they don't fall victim to some common dangers of the internet. It's worth noting too that there are federal laws such as the Children's Online Privacy Protection Act (COPPA), that have been enacted to protect kids when online. COPPA applies to children younger than 13 and it requires websites to explain their privacy policies and get parental consent before collecting or using a child's personal information. Importantly, it prohibits sites from demanding children to provide excess personal information to play a game. Like on some websites as soon as one inputs his or her age, they are restricted to what their age can contain or carry. Adult stuffs are barred from the underaged. However, laws are sometimes broken online, hence you must put up a strong and best defense while working online. One of the prevalent dangers of the internet is cybercriminals and the ever-evolving cybercrimes they create. To protect your family members from cyber-attacks you have to drill your kids on what and what not to expect when online. Save yourself a fortune by investing in cyber safety. There are many threats children face online, as well as adults and teens. Internet Education for the whole family on how to identify and avoid each cyberthreat is an important part of internet safety. Cybersecurity uses techniques that help in securing digital components, data, network and computer systems from unauthorized digital access. Below are some of the internet threats you should be aware of:

Identity theft
Cyberbullying
Online predators
Faulty privacy setting
Phishing
Online scams
Malware (trojan, spyware, adware etc.)
Inappropriate content
Bait and switch

- Most of these internet threats and the way out are explained in subsequent chapters.

2 TYPES OF CYBERCRIMES OR ATTACKS 1

Types of Cyber Crimes or attacks
- Malware (malicious software) Attacks:
A malware attack is a common cyberattack where malware executes unauthorized actions on the victim's system. Malware is a blanket term for viruses, worms, trojans and other harmful computer programs The malicious software encompasses many specific types of attacks such as ransomware, spyware, command and control, and more. Here we have different types like covid Lock, ransomware, trojan, crypto Locker, worm, etc. Malware typically infects a machine by tricking users into clicking and/or installing a program that they shouldn't from the Internet. The most common malware attack involves viruses. A virus infects a system when a user clicks unwarranted links or installs a software from suspicious source. Most viruses self-replicate without the knowledge of the user and cause havoc or damage to a system and its network. Hackers use it to steal passwords, delete files and render computers inoperable.

- Anti-malware. Cybersecurity for home and businesses Malwarebytes can protect you against malware, ransomware, malicious websites, and other advanced online threats that have made traditional antivirus obsolete. Antimalware is a type of software program created to protect information technology (IT) systems and individual computers from malicious software, or malware. Such programs scan a computer system to prevent, detect and remove malware. Comodo for example contains BOClean Anti-Malware Protection Software. It's an advanced security feature that destroys malware as soon as it enters the computer. Trend Micro has a sandbox where suspicious files are analyzed. Kaspersky has a Security Cloud that adapts to your browsing habits to keep you protected. Antimalware focuses on new threats, while antivirus keeps you protected against the traditional versions, like worms and phishing attacks, that can still harm your device. Antivirus

3

offer proactive protection, acting in advance to deal with threats infecting your device while antimalware roots and destroys activated malware.

- Phishing:

Phishing is a type of social engineering attack often used to steal user data, including login credentials and credit card numbers. It occurs when an attacker, undercover pretending to be a trusted entity, deceives a victim into opening an email, instant message, or text message. Examples of phishing attacks are:

Spear Phishing: Spear phishing is an email or electronic communications scam targeted towards a specific individual, organization or business to steal data and install malware on their computer.

- Link Manipulation: Link manipulation occurs when an application embeds user input into the path or domain of URLs that appear within application responses

- Fake Websites: A website built for purposes of committing fraud. Like in cloning a genuine website to deceive a victim into revealing sensitive information, or to purchase products that never exist or never arrives at buyers address when purchased or to download some form of malware.

- CEO Fraud: CEO Fraud is a scam in which cybercriminals spoof company email accounts and impersonate executives to try and fool an employee in accounting or HR into carrying out fraud

- Content Injection: Content Injection, otherwise known as Content Spoofing, is the act of manipulating what a user sees on a site by adding parameters to their URL. This act is a known form of attack on a website. While Content Injection and XSS (Cross Site Scripting) Attacks are similar, they differ in a few key ways.

- Session Hijacking: Session hijacking is as the term suggests. A user in a session can be hijacked by an attacker and lose control of the session altogether, where their personal data can easily be stolen. After a user starts a session, such as logging into a banking website, an attacker can hijack it.

- Whaling: Whaling is a highly targeted phishing attack - aimed at senior executives - masquerading as a legitimate email. Whaling is digitally enabled fraud through social engineering, designed to encourage victims to perform a secondary action, such as initiating a wire transfer of funds.

- Vishing: This is the fraudulent practice of making phone calls or leaving voice messages purporting to be from reputable companies in order to induce individuals to reveal personal information, such as bank details and credit card numbers.

Email Phishing. The word phishing was coined around 1996 by hackers stealing America Online accounts and passwords. These internet scammers were using e-mail lures, setting out hooks to "fish" for passwords and financial data from the "sea" of Internet users.

- Man in the Middle Attack (MITM):

A man-in-the-middle attack is a type of eavesdropping attack, where attackers interrupt an existing conversation or data transfer. After inserting themselves in the "middle" of the transfer, the attackers pretend to be both legitimate participants.

- To prevent this middle man, use a Virtual Private Network (VPN) to encrypt your web traffic. An encrypted VPN severely limits a hacker's ability to read or modify web traffic. Be prepared to prevent data loss; have a cyber security incident response plan. One example of a MITM attack is active eavesdropping, in which the attacker makes independent connections with the victims and relays messages between them.

- You can install firewalls between your device and the internet. It could be software or hardwires which filters incoming traffic. Also, you could also install what is called honeypot. Honeypot trap is a security mechanism that creates a virtual trap to lure attackers. An intentionally compromised dummy computer system allowing attackers to exploit vulnerabilities so you can study them to improve your security policies. In espionage CIA Honeypot females are used in disguise to lure enemies. Just like honey attract bees honeypot attract cyber attackers deceiving them into believing they are the real thing or target thereby shielding the main system from attackers.

- Password Attacks:
  Types of password attacks are:
- Phishing Attacks
- Credential Stuffing Attacks
- Brute Force Attacks
- Dictionary Attacks
- Password Spraying Attacks
- Keylogger Attacks
- Man in the middle attack

Brute-Force Attack. A brute-force attack is a type of password attack where hackers make numerous hit-or-miss attempts to gain access. Protect yourself from password attacks There are lots of password cracking programs on the internet, each with their own special recipe, but they all basically do one of two things: create variations from a dictionary of known common passwords or attempt every possible combination using a method called a brute force
attack.

- Prevent this by making passwords that are hard to guess. Use random letter, word, symbol, and number combinations so your passwords aren't at risk of a brute force attack.

- Social Engineering

Social engineering preys on human emotions. It is the term used for a broad range of malicious activities accomplished through human interactions. It uses psychological manipulation to trick users into making security mistakes or giving away sensitive information. Social engineering attacks happen in one or more steps. Social engineering is the art of manipulating people so they give up confidential information.

- Dos Attack

A Denial-of-Service (DoS) attack is an attack meant to shut down a machine or network, making it inaccessible to its intended users. DoS attacks accomplish this by flooding the target with traffic, or sending in information that triggers a crash.

- To prevent this, strengthen your network security by fortifying all internet-facing devices to prevent compromise, installing and maintaining antivirus software, establishing firewalls.

- SQL Attack

SQL is a query language. SQL injection attack, also known as SQLI, is a common attack vector that uses malicious SQL code for backend database manipulation to access information that was not intended to be displayed like sensitive company data, user lists or private customer details. Cyber attacker sends his evil content triggering malicious SQL commands to be executed in the database. They can edit add remove tables from databases.

- Network Attack

These are infiltration of unauthorized actions on the digital assets within an organizational network. The attacks could be passive where network attacks, malicious parties gain unauthorized access to networks, monitor, and steal private data without making any alterations or active.

3 TYPES OF CYBERCRIMES OR ATTACKS 2

- Identity Theft:

Identity theft is the crime of obtaining the personal or financial information of another person to use their identity to commit fraud, such as making unauthorized transactions or purchases. There are different types of identity theft which include financial identity theft,

tax identity theft,

medical identity theft,

employment identity theft,

child identity theft,

senior identity theft.

Such information is extracted through various ways like browsing through trash can, uncleared cookies, unsecure websites to accessing databases.

- What do you do if you are a victim of identity theft?

You can file a claim with your identity theft insurance, if applicable. Notify your bank, business partners, companies of your stolen identity. File a report with the Federal Trade Commission (FTC) online at IdentityTheft.gov or by phone at 1-877-438-4338. The FTC will collect the details of your situation. Contact also your local police department. Place a fraud alert on your credit reports. Freeze your credit. You can also employ a credit monitoring service.

How can I find out if someone is using my identity?

- Track your bills and when they're due. If you stop getting a bill, that could be a sign that someone changed your billing address. Check your bank account statement. Review your credit reports.

- To see if someone is using your SSN for employment purposes, review your Social Security Statement at www.socialsecurity.gov/myaccount to look for suspicious activity. Also regularly check your bank and credit card accounts online.

- Check your bank account for unusual transactions. Look out for unusual emails, texts, and letters.

- Ransomware:

Victims of ransomware are mainly people using outdated software or who don't update their apps. Updates or upgrades could counter new or known threats. Cyber criminals employ malware or codes that encrypt your data or stored information making it hard for you to access your information. They send you a code on how to unlock them at a price. Evil world! Paying ransom to attackers to get access to your own information. Lock and encrypt a victim's computer or device data, then demand a ransom to restore access. In many cases, the victim must pay the cybercriminal within a set amount of time or risk losing access forever. Holding a victim's information at ransom. A user or organization's important data (files, database, applications) is encrypted so that they cannot access it. Ransomware is often designed to spread across a network and target database and file servers, and can thus quickly paralyze an entire organization. It is a growing threat, generating billions of dollars to cybercriminals and inflicting significant damage and expenses for businesses and governmental organizations.

- Ransomware uses asymmetric encryption. This is cryptography that uses a pair of keys to encrypt and decrypt a file. The public-private pair of keys is uniquely generated by the attacker for the victim, with the private key to decrypt the files stored on the attacker's server. The attacker makes the private key available to the victim only after the ransom is paid, though as seen in recent ransomware campaigns, that is not always the case. Without access to the private key, it is nearly impossible to decrypt the files that are being held for ransom. The example of the spring of 2017 WannaCry outbreak, which afflicted over 200,000 computers in over 150 countries comes to mind. It costed the UK £92 million and running up global costs of up to £6 billion.

- How to Fix Ransomware: Ransomware engineers use techniques involving phishing and social engineering to make it harder for potential victims to discern if an email or link would direct them to a possible ransomware attack. The secrecy and privacy of cryptocurrency help attackers hide their Identity or loot. What do you do to bypass the ransom note on your screen?

1. Restart Your Computer.

2. Press the F8 key while your computer is booting up.

3. Use the arrow keys to select the Safe Mode option on the screen.

4. Type rstrui.exe using the text cursor that appears on the screen

5. Press Enter.

6. In the Windows System Restore screen, choose a date and restore your computer to this point.

7. Using another device, download a good anti ransomware attacks software.

8. Copy the software installer file and install it on infected device.

9. Run a full scan.

10. Select all infections detected by the ransomware and delete them from your computer.

- If you have a backup copy of all your files, you can just then copy then back to the cleansed device. If no backup files, use a recovery software to recover deleted files in your computer. During a ransomware attack, your actual files will be deleted by the malware and will be replaced by an encrypted replica. That gives you a chance to retrieve lost data by using a data recovery software.

- Free online decryption tools can be used to unlock at least some of the ransomware-locked data, if not all.

Protect your computer before the doom day from ransomware attackers. Prevention they say is better or cheaper than cure.

- Keystroke logging or Keylogging:

Keystroke logging, often referred to as keylogging or keyboard capturing, is the action of recording (logging) the keys struck on a keyboard, typically covertly, so that a person using the keyboard is unaware that their actions are being monitored. Keyloggers secretly record what you see, say and do on your computer. Employers use it to watch employees, but cybercriminals use them too. You can detect keyloggers on Android by checking the application manager. Application downloads outside Google Play Store are likely to carry keylogger infection. Keyloggers give hackers access to your personal data - passwords, credit card numbers, webpages visited. Use of Keylogger is unlawful if used for criminal purposes. We have software keyloggers and hardware keyloggers. So be careful what you type when using unprotected systems in public places like in Airports, public library etc.

- Bait and Switch:

Bait and Switch is an advertising scams or common deceptive sales practice that advertises or offer low price to attract customers but when they come the price is changed or product is not available and the customer is directed to an expensive alternative.

- You can escape this by reading the terms and conditions, comparing with other Sellers, clarifying the Pricing terms, not agree to a purchase if you feel uncomfortable.

- You can report the advisers by first submitting a consumer report to the FTC, which you can do by filling out an online form. The FTC will investigate the complaint and take action against the seller if they find evidence that bait and switch tactics were being used.

4 ETHICAL HACKING

- **Ethical hacking** is a process of detecting vulnerabilities in an application, system, or organization's infrastructure that an attacker can use to exploit an individual or organization. They use this process to prevent cyberattacks and security breaches by lawfully hacking into the systems and looking for weak points. We have 3 types of hackers?

- **Ethical Hacker.**

They hack officially, to locate vulnerabilities, and providing solutions to fix them and ensure safety. Not for fraud or abuse and are done by trained qualified cybersecurity certified experts. This specialty is a fast-growing course worldwide now. It is also called white hat hacker

- **Non-Ethical Hacker.**

Non-ethical hackers perform hacking for criminal purposes. They break into people's digital world and systems, phishing and vishing, attacking and sabotaging. It is also called by some black hat hacker

- **Grey Hat Hacker.**

Grey hat hackers are the combination of ethical and non-ethical hackers. They hack without any malicious intention, just for fun. They are unauthorized hackers too since they have no approval from the targeted organization.

Ethical hacking is lawful and used to checkmate the activities of hackers. Instances of intelligence gathering is the first stage of hacking. It is like using the activities or trail left by the hacker to track them. The Certified Ethical Hacker and cyber security professional are employed by organization to provide periodic checks and safety for their online systems. Ethical hacking is also referred to as penetration testing, intrusion testing and red teaming. A white hat ethical hacker is a computer security expert, who specializes in penetration testing and other testing methodologies. They see to the protection of organization's information systems.

- Processes of ethical hacking are:

1. Reconnaissance - the footprint or information gathering phase. Preliminary survey

2. Scanning - here attackers try to find different ways to gain the target's information like user accounts, credentials, IP addresses, etc.

3. Gaining Access - here attacker uses all means to get unauthorized access to the target's systems, applications, or networks.

4. Maintaining Access - he maintains access and continuously exploits the system using various tools to steal data.

5. Clearing Track - this last stage involves clearing their tracks so as not to be detected, using reverse HTTP Shells, deleting cache and history to erase the digital footprint.

5 HOW TO PROTECT YOUR DATA

- **Update and upgrade security software** patches regularly
- **Use verified antivirus software**. Some free anti-virus might be ploy of hackers like in most freebies to introduce hidden malwares like trojan, adware or spywares into your system
- **Use Cloud Computing** for backing up critical data.
- If you backup your data offline no one will hold you to random, not even a ransomware attacker. Ransomware attack can be destructive if you don't have a backup of your data. Protect your data.
- **A password manager**, like 1Password or LastPass will offer a more secure way to create strong passwords and better storage for them. Browsers like Safari and Chrome offer built-in password managers. Update your passwords. Use password generator in your password manager, to create strong passwords for every account.
- **Use two-way verification authentication** for important accounts. In addition to your password in logging in, you receive a code to your registered phone number to confirm that you are the authentic user.
- **In browsing use trusted devices**, strong alpha-numeric passwords, private incognito mode, clear browsing history and cookies before you leave. In public computers avoid opening sensitive accounts like your bank accounts. Use your bank apps rather. Beware of clone websites. Be sure of secure browsers with the locked green padlock at top left and that the "https://" not "http://", (hypertext transfer protocol with an "s" meaning Secured) starts the website URL (Uniform resource locator) address you type in or visited.
- **Update your apps and** buy verified software. Freebies sometimes come with risk. Updates and upgrades come with new protections against new threats to your devices. Evil people and their vices don't sleep. They are always ahead.

- **Secure your own Wi-Fi network**, hotspots, routers and systems. Make sure you're using a WPA2 password (Wi-Fi password)

- **Use a VPN (virtual Private Network)** like Proton, Atlas to protect your data. A VPN provides you with a temporary IP address and encrypts your web browsing activity so that even if a hacker gains access to the public Wi-Fi network, they won't be able to steal your data.

- **Defeat Phishing scams by examining the message**. They try to drive you into panic so you act quick. Check sender email which is hidden under the more… link and be sure it is actually from the purported sender. If not, if it is from another domain or one or few symbol were added to the real original email address to deceive you, click it as scam in your email box. If still in doubt call your bank directly, and ask if the email is legitimate. Do not click on any suspicious links, download any files, or call any phone numbers associated with the potential phishing email.

- **Use a spam filter** provided by your email provider. It will reduce the frequency of such mails.

- **While making payment online** avoid using debit cards if possible as it is linked directly to your bank account. Rather use third-party payment method like PayPal, Apple Pay, Google Pay or a credit card as these third-party payment method offers a layer of protection against fraud. Often check your bank and credit card statements, as well as your credit report, for suspicious activities and make report to relevant authorities where necessary

Online Dating: Cat-fishers (romance or dating pretenders) use their dating or social media platforms to extract sensitive information from their victims. So, so- called lovers have lost lots of money from such unholy relationships and pretenders.

6 INTERNET SAFETY TIPS FOR KIDS AND TEENS

Internet safety tips for kids

As kids grow up, they get involved in learning processes whether at school or outside the school environment. Virtually, in game centers, watching YouTube, or in other digital based learning processes and centers So, it's important to teach children earlier enough some internet safety tips. Kids should

- Be aware of the dangers of the internet. Teach kids on how to recognize suspicious activities online and when in doubt to ask for help.

- Remember not to disclose personal information like social security number, home address, passwords, date of birth, family details online without the supervision of their parents. Scammers can trick kids into disclosing their Social Security number and other details that can be used to commit identity theft.

- Beware of strangers. Teach children to be cautious of divulging personal information like social security number, date of birth, home address etc. online or to strangers without the supervision of parents or adults. Scammer can steal such vital information from them at games or children's websites. This is identity theft

- Watch out for phishing

You may be sophisticated enough to know not to click on a URL that's supposedly from your bank or a friend, but does everyone in your household know that? Teach your kids about phishing scams and warn them not to click on URLs in an email or social network message.

What is cyberbullying?

Cyberbullying is simple acts in cyberspace intended to make life unbearable or unpleasant for others. It is also same as bullying online, cyber-harassment, harassment online, online bullying, online harassment. It is bullying with the use of digital technologies. It can take place on social media, messaging platforms, gaming platforms and mobile phones. Cyberbullies repeatedly carry out threats, scaring, angering or shaming their victims or targets. Instances of spreading lies about or posting embarrassing photos of someone on social media, sending hurtful messages, impersonation and sending mean messages to others on behalf of their targets. But cyberbullying leaves a digital footprint traceable to the attacker. This can be used to stop the abuse.

- if you feel threatened speak to your parents or adults or visit Child Helpline International for help.

- UNICEF (extract from https://www.unicef.org/end-violence/how-to-stop-cyberbullying) provided answers as shown below to these 10 popular questions about cyberbullying.

1. Am I being bullied online? How do you tell the difference between a joke and bullying?

2. What are the effects of cyberbullying?

3. Who should I talk to if someone is bullying me online? Why is reporting important?

4. I'm experiencing cyberbullying, but I'm afraid to talk to my parents about it. How can I approach them?

5. How can I help my friends report a case of cyberbullying especially if they don't want to do it?

6. How do we stop cyberbullying without giving up access to the internet?

7. How do I prevent my personal information from being used to manipulate or humiliate me on social media?

8. Is there a punishment for cyberbullying?

9. Internet companies don't seem to care about online bullying and harassment. Are they being held responsible?

10. Are there any online anti-bullying tools for children or young people?

UNICEF RESPONSE:

1. Am I being bullied online? How do you tell the difference between a joke and bullying?

UNICEF:

All friends joke around with each other, but sometimes it's hard to tell if someone is just having fun or trying to hurt you, especially online. Sometimes they'll laugh it off with a "just kidding," or "don't take it so seriously." But if you feel hurt or think others are laughing at you instead of with you, then the joke has gone too far. If it continues even after you've asked the person to stop and you are still feeling upset about it, then this could be bullying.

And when the bullying takes place online, it can result in unwanted attention from a wide range of people including strangers. Wherever it may happen, if you are not happy about it, you should not have to stand for it. Call it what you will – if you feel bad and it doesn't stop, then it's worth getting help. Stopping cyberbullying is not just about calling out bullies, it's also about recognizing that everyone deserves respect online and in real life.

2. What are the effects of cyberbullying?

UNICEF:

When bullying happens online it can feel as if you're being attacked everywhere, even inside your own home. It can seem like there's no escape. The effects can last a long time and affect a person in many ways:

Mentally — feeling upset, embarrassed, stupid, even angry

-Emotionally — feeling ashamed or losing interest in the things you love

Physically — tired (loss of sleep), or experiencing symptoms like stomach aches and headaches

The feeling of being laughed at or harassed by others, can prevent people from speaking up or trying to deal with the problem. In extreme cases, cyberbullying can even lead to people taking their own lives.

Cyberbullying can affect us in many ways. But these can be overcome and people can regain their confidence and health.

3. Who should I talk to if someone is bullying me online? Why is reporting important?

UNICEF:

If you think you're being bullied, the first step is to seek help from someone you trust such as your parents, a close family member or another trusted adult. In your school you can reach out to a counsellor, the sports coach or your favorite teacher. And if you are not comfortable talking to someone you know, search for a helpline in your country to talk to a professional counsellor. If the bullying is happening on a social platform, consider blocking the bully and formally reporting their behavior on the platform itself. Social media companies are obligated to keep their users safe. It can be helpful to collect evidence – text messages and screen shots of social media posts – to show what's been going on. For bullying to stop, it needs to be identified and reporting it is key. It can also help to show the bully that their behavior is unacceptable.

- If you are in immediate danger, then you should contact the police or emergency services in your country.

- For bullying to stop, it needs to be identified and reporting it is key.

- Facebook/Instagram:

If you're being bullied online, we encourage you to talk to a parent, teacher or someone else you can trust - You have a right to be safe. We also make it easy to report any bullying directly within Facebook or Instagram.

You can always send our team an anonymous report from a post, comment or story on Facebook or Instagram.

We have a team who reviews these reports 24/7 around the world in 50+ languages, and we'll remove anything that's abusive or bullying. These reports are always anonymous. We have a guide on Facebook that can help lead you through the process of dealing with bullying -- or what to do if you see someone else being bullied. On Instagram, we also have a Parent's Guide that provides recommendations for parents, guardians and trusted adults on how to navigate cyberbullying, and a central hub where you can learn about our safety tools.

Twitter:

If you think that you are being cyberbullied, the most important thing is to ensure you are safe. It's essential to have someone to talk to about what you are going through. This may be a teacher, another trusted adult, or a parent. Talk to your parents and friends about what to do if you or a friend are being cyberbullied. We encourage people to report accounts to us that may break our rules. You can do this through the support pages on our Help Center or through the in-Tweet reporting mechanism by clicking on the "Report a Tweet" option.

4. I'm experiencing cyberbullying, but I'm afraid to talk to my parents about it. How can I approach them?

UNICEF:

If you are experiencing cyberbullying, speaking to a trusted adult – someone you feel safe talking to – is one of the most important first steps you can take.

Talking to parents isn't easy for everyone. But there are things you can do to help the conversation. Choose a time to talk when you know you have their full attention. Explain how serious the problem is for you. Remember, they might not be as familiar with technology as you are, so you might need to help them to understand what's happening. They might not have instant answers for you, but they are likely to want to help and together you can find a solution.

Two heads are always better than one! If you are still unsure about what to do, consider reaching out to other trusted people. There are often more people who care about you and are willing to help than you might think!

5. How can I help my friends report a case of cyberbullying especially if they don't want to do it?

UNICEF:

Anyone can become a victim of cyberbullying. If you see this happening to someone you know, try to offer support. It is important to listen to your friend. Why don't they want to report being cyberbullied? How are they feeling? Let them know that they don't have to formally report anything, but it's crucial to talk to someone who might be able to help. Remember, your friend may be feeling fragile. Be kind to them. Help them think through what they might say and to whom. Offer to go with them if they decide to report. Most importantly, remind them that you're there for them and you want to help. If your friend still does not want to report the incident, then support them in finding a trusted adult who can help them deal with the situation. Remember that in certain situations the consequences of cyberbullying can be life threatening.

Doing nothing can leave the person feeling that everyone is against them or that nobody cares. Your words can make a difference.

Anyone can become a victim of cyberbullying.

Facebook/Instagram:

We know that it can be hard to report someone. But, it's never OK to bully anyone.

Reporting content to Facebook or Instagram can help us better keep you safe on our platforms. Bullying and harassment are highly personal by nature, so in many instances, we need a person to report this behavior to us before we can identify or remove it.

Reporting a case of cyberbullying is always anonymous on Instagram and Facebook, and no one will ever know you let us know about this behavior.

You can report something you experience yourself, but it's also just as easy to report for one of your friends using the tools available directly in the app. More information on how to report something is included in Instagram's Help Center and on Facebook's Help Center.

You could also let your friend know about a tool on Instagram called Restrict, where you can discreetly protect your account without having to block someone - which can seem harsh for some people.

Twitter:

We enabled bystander reporting which means that you can make a report on behalf of another person. This can now be done for reports of private information and impersonation as well.

6. How do we stop cyberbullying without giving up access to the Internet?

UNICEF:

Being online has so many benefits. However, like many things in life, it comes with risks that you need to protect against. If you experience cyberbullying, you may want to delete certain apps or stay offline for a while to give yourself time to recover. But getting off the Internet is not a long-term solution. You did nothing wrong, so why should you be disadvantaged? It may even send the bullies the wrong signal — encouraging their unacceptable behavior.

We all want cyberbullying to stop, which is one of the reasons reporting cyberbullying is so important. But creating the Internet we want to go beyond calling out bullying. We need to be thoughtful about what we share or say that may hurt others. We need to be kind to one another online and in real life. It's up to all of us! We need to be thoughtful about what we share or say that may hurt others.

Facebook/Instagram:

Keeping Instagram and Facebook safe and positive places for self-expression is important to us -- people will only be comfortable sharing if they feel safe. But we know that cyberbullying can get in the way and create negative experiences. That's why at Instagram and Facebook, we're committed to leading the fight against cyberbullying.

We're doing this in two main ways. First, by using technology to prevent people from experiencing and seeing bullying. For example, people can turn on a setting that uses artificial intelligence technology to automatically filter and hide bullying comments intended to harass or upset people.

Second, we're working to encourage positive behavior and interactions by giving people tools to customize their experience on Facebook and Instagram. Restrict is one tool designed to empower you to discreetly protect your account while still keeping an eye on a bully.

Twitter:

Since hundreds of millions of people share ideas on Twitter, it's no surprise that we don't all agree. That's one of the benefits because we can all learn from respectful disagreements and discussions.

But sometimes, after you've listened to someone for a while, you may not want to hear them anymore. Their right to express themselves doesn't mean you're required to listen.

7. How do I prevent my personal information from being used to manipulate or humiliate me on social media?

UNICEF:

Think twice before posting or sharing anything online – it may stay online forever and could be used to harm you later. Don't give out personal details such as your address, telephone number or the name of your school.

Learn about the privacy settings of your favorite social media apps. Here are some actions you can take on many of them: You can decide who can see your profile, send you direct messages or comment on your posts by adjusting your account privacy settings.

You can report hurtful comments, messages and photos and request they be removed.

Besides 'unfriending', you can completely block people to stop them from seeing your profile or contacting you.

You can also choose to have comments by certain people to appear only to them without completely blocking them.

You can delete posts on your profile or hide them from specific people.

On most of your favorite social media, people aren't notified when you block, restrict or report them.

8. Is there a punishment for cyberbullying?

UNICEF:

Most schools take bullying seriously and will take action against it. If you are being cyberbullied by other students, report it to your school.

People who are victims of any form of violence, including bullying and cyberbullying, have a right to justice and to have the offender held accountable.

Laws against bullying, particularly on cyberbullying, are relatively new and still do not exist everywhere. This is why many countries rely on other relevant laws, such as ones against harassment, to punish cyberbullies.

In countries that have specific laws on cyberbullying, online behavior that deliberately causes serious emotional distress is seen as criminal activity. In some of these countries, victims of cyberbullying can seek protection, prohibit communication from a specified person and restrict the use of electronic devices used by that person for cyberbullying, temporarily or permanently.

However, it is important to remember that punishment is not always the most effective way to change the behavior of bullies. It is often better to focus on repairing the harm and mending the relationship.

Facebook/Instagram:

On Facebook, we have a set of Community Standards, and on Instagram, we have Community Guidelines that we ask our community to follow. If we find content that violates these policies, like in the case of bullying or harassment, we'll remove it.

If you think content has been removed incorrectly, we also allow for appeals. On Instagram, you can appeal content or account removal through our Help Center. On Facebook, you can also go through the same process on the Help Center.

Twitter:

We strongly enforce our rules to ensure all people can participate in the public conversation freely and safely. These rules specifically cover a number of areas including topics such as:

- Violence
- Child sexual exploitation
- Abuse/harassment
- Hateful conduct
- Suicide or self-harm
- Sensitive media, including graphic violence and adult content

As part of these rules, we take a number of different enforcement actions when content is in violation. When we take enforcement actions, we may do so either on a specific piece of content (e.g., an individual Tweet or Direct Message) or on an account. You can find more on our enforcement actions here.

9. Internet companies don't seem to care about online bullying and harassment. Are they being held responsible?

UNICEF:

Internet companies are increasingly paying attention to the issue of online bullying.

Many of them are introducing ways to address it and better protect their users with new tools, guidance and ways to report online abuse.

But it is true that even more is needed. Many young people experience cyberbullying every day. Some face extreme forms of online abuse. Some have taken their own lives as a result.

Technology companies have a responsibility to protect their users especially children and young people.

It is up to all of us to hold them accountable when they're not living up to these responsibilities.

10. Are there any online anti-bullying tools for children or young people?
UNICEF:

Each social platform offers different tools (see available ones below) that allow you to restrict who can comment on or view your posts or who can connect automatically as a friend, and to report cases of bullying. Many of them involve simple steps to block, mute or report cyberbullying. We encourage you to explore them.

Social media companies also provide educational tools and guidance for children, parents and teachers to learn about risks and ways to stay safe online.

Also, the first line of defense against cyberbullying could be you. Think about where cyberbullying happens in your community and ways you can help – by raising your voice, calling out bullies, reaching out to trusted adults or by creating awareness of the issue. Even a simple act of kindness can go a long way.

If you are worried about your safety or something that has happened to you online, urgently speak to an adult you trust. Many countries have a special helpline you can call for free and talk to someone anonymously. Visit Child Helpline International to find help in your country.

- The first line of defense against cyberbullying could be you.

Facebook/Instagram:
We have a number of tools to help keep young people safe:

-You can opt to ignore all messages from a bully or use our Restrict tool to discreetly protect your account without that person being notified.

- You can moderate comments on your own posts.

- You can modify your settings so that only people you follow can send you a direct message.

- And on Instagram, we send you a notification you're about to post something that might cross the line, encouraging you to reconsider.

For more tips on how to protect yourself and others from cyberbullying, check out our resources on Facebook or Instagram.

Twitter:
If people on Twitter become annoying or negative, we have tools that can help you, and the following list is linked to instructions on how to set these up.

- Mute - removing an account's Tweets from your timeline without unfollowing or blocking that account.

- Block - restricting specific accounts from contacting you, seeing your Tweets, and following you.

- Report - filing a report about abusive behavior

*****

Internet safety tips for teens

Some teenagers may be more tech savvy than their parents, but have low sense of judgment. Adults should help teach teenagers and even young adults internet safety tips like these:

- Choose strong passwords

How do you create a strong password? Choosing wrong or weak easy-to-remember passwords like 123456 or qwerty make you and your system vulnerable. The first six figures on your keyboard or the first direct letters QWERTY facing you on your keyboard. You make it easy for hackers to attack your account. Password should be a mixture of small and capital letters, figures and symbols and not necessarily birthdays which could be seen anywhere. Data breach (a process that connects two or more stable, predefined data stores for a limited time or on an ongoing basis, used in a variety of applications) has exposed millions of people's personal info. online. Election data of countries, big organizations databases, etc. Passwords are the primary defense against hackers. Yet, many people reuse the same password for multiple accounts and use passwords that are easy to guess, because they're also easy to remember. Teach your kids to create a hack-proof password by selecting a combination of uppercase and lowercase letters, numbers, and symbols, and make sure it's at least 12 characters long. Never use common words, phrases, or personal information like a phone number or family members' names.

- Use a password management program, which can remember unique passwords for all your accounts. With a password manager you can organize and protect to your passwords.

- **Protect your social media** accounts from cyber snoops and identity thieves. Parents should remind teens to also be wary of strangers who ask for their details.

- Be careful what you post. It's important for children, teens, and family members to know what they give out online in order to prove a point or express themselves. Details of documents like driver's license, personal photos, travel documents, home addresses could be dangerous and expose the family or attract online predators

- **Shop online only from secure sites**. Check out your browser for a green padlock top left and on the address bar a web address starting with https (hypertext transfer protocol with an s meaning secured). Of course, parents determine whether to allow their children shop online or supervise them. They say it is unethical to promote your product or advertise to kids.

- **Use privacy settings on your browser** when shopping online. In chrome browser is called incognito and gives you a black background when on. This protects your privacy because whatever you type in is not stored as cookies or history after your session.

- **Personal Information**. Do not share your last name, home address, school name, or telephone number without consent of your parents.

- In social medias, social networking, game sites or in using screen names online do not include personal information such as last name or date of birth.

- **Passwords**. Your passwords is your secret and must not be divulge to anyone. Always logout after any session online especially when you use public computers like in libraries. If possible, delete cookies and browser history before you leave.

- **Photos**. Be careful what photos or digitals you post online. Always tell your parents

- Ask your parents advice if an online friend want to meet you offline. You cannot trust a stranger's intentions. Kidnappers, ritualists, cybercriminals, spies, all use the same internet.

- If you must shop online do that under the supervision of your parents or a internet savvy known adult. This is to avoid entering the trap of fraudsters. Avoid clicking suspicious links especially those offering freebies because they could be a trick to extract vital information details that will turn to harm you.

- **Beware of download links**, especially for free apps, or email attachments you don't know the sender. Your

downloads might contain virus or malwares like Trojan horse, adware or spyware which puts you and your device in harm's way.

- **Ignore cyberbullies** who send anonymous threats or insults. Report to your teacher or parents if you know them and they persist with their threats or insults.

- **During research** for school work consult your librarian, parents, or your teacher for safe websites.

7 INTERNET SAFETY TIPS FOR PARENTS AND THE WHOLE FAMILY

Internet safety tips for parents

Some parent's stuffs are out of the way of kids and are needed to protect the household.

- Supervise your family online. Children are vulnerable even when they think they are clever or know more than their parents. Yes, some teenagers may know more internet stuff but may not manage that knowledge hence they fall prey to the more sophisticated hackers. Whose problem then? None other than the parents and the wider family.

Family Discussion tips

- Let the Kid teach you!

By allowing your child to teach you, you can see and identify the problem areas like privacy settings and level of security measures.

- Watch a video or movies about children online challenges. Raise a topic or open a discussion from what your whole family have watched

- Know how they use internet or tech - playing games or chatting. Your interest will create good rapport that when confused the come to you for help.

- From here the family values are made known to all the family members and how to protect it online and elsewhere. Let them to think before they post anything and how it could affect them and others

- Suggest they search themselves online and see what reputation.

- Make sure your child's profile is set to private for some control.

- Sexting: this is the sharing of sexually explicit images or messages. Discourage kids from such inappropriate or even illegality online or over mobile devices.

- Discourage the use of pornography

- For 10-year-old and under supervise their use of internet.

- Children in their tween years may want freedom. Let them do so in private mode.

- For teenagers let them know about safe search. They will want to explore everything.

- **Online Grooming** is where online an adult contacts like a 16-year for sexual activity (child sex abuse). The offender uses fictitious name posing to be of same age with the victim. Police will even have no evidence.

- parents look out for potential warning like aggressive and secretive behavior when questioned about their online activities.

- Unexplained gifts or cash in your child's possession

Language type change like use of sexual language

- Make sure your child's online friends are known to you.

Warn them about receiving free gifts. They say nothing is free. Even in Freetown they say there's no free food.

- Talk about sex and sexuality. Help them develop strategies for saying no to sexual solicitations from people online.

- Teach them on how to block and report abusive and unwanted people on the sites and applications they use.

- **In cyberbullying** If your child is the one bullying others, he may have some emotional problem. Find out why he is doing so and explain to him or her why bullying is unacceptable.

- **Understand privacy policies.**

They say nothing is private even with private browsers because there are many documents, we consent to online without reading them. It is good you read these agreements and policies so you know what you are signing.

- **Backup data regularly** so that if by accident you lose your data you can replace them. Or if you have ransomware attack you can be able to recover your system and to replace your data.

- **Use VPN** (virtual private network) like Proton, Atlas to Keep your internet connection secure

- You can monitor your kids online activities or block them out of adult sites by installing some software or using some cybersecurity tools with parental controls on your kids' devices to block certain features on games, track kids' location, backup their data, and manage their screen time.

- **Install a comprehensive cybersecurity suite**

that provides protection for all your family members and their devices such as smartphone, tablet, laptops, smart doorbell, home security system, and other internet-connected devices.

- Seek support from experts or online where necessary.

- Internet safety tips for the whole family

- Downloads especially from untrusted sites or sources could be dangerous. Run security checks before downloading especially free stuff.

Hackers plant malwares in some of these downloads and they are installed in your system as well.

- Go private on public Wi-Fi by using VPN

- Close unused accounts as they could be fertile ground for cybercriminals to extract private information.

- E-Security Tips

How do I restrict Internet access to my child?

Find your child's name and click Content restrictions. Scroll to Web browsing and toggle Block inappropriate websites from off to On. For blocking specific sites, add their URLs under Always blocked. To limit your child to only browse specific websites, check the box next to Only allow these websites.

- Parental control or monitoring apps or software

These software and hardware solutions let you block unwanted web content, limit screen time, restrict the use of risky applications, and more. Basically, they are a way to help keep your kids safer on their computers and mobile devices. Communicate with your kids before implementing any of these options, as it is important that they feel that you respect their privacy. Otherwise, they'll make sure to find a way around any protections, even if you had your kids' best interests in mind.

- **Parental control app Qustodio** is a highly configurable, easy-to-manage tool for keeping track of your child's activity on Windows, macOS, Chromebook, iOS, Android, and even Kindle devices, though it is expensive.

- **Kaspersky Safe Kids** is a full-featured, affordable parental monitoring system for desktop and mobile platforms that doesn't impose limits on the number of devices you can monitor.

- **Parental control device Circle Home Plus** delivers good tools for keeping an eye on your home network and protecting your children's phones and tablets, but it is susceptible to workarounds and its reporting features aren't as robust as competitors'.

- **Locategy's parental control app** for Android and iOS keeps track of your kid's activities and location, but the apps are missing social media monitoring of any kind and there's no support for Macs or PCs.

- **Mobicip** gives you the basic tools you need to monitor your children's web and app activity, but the lack of sophisticated time- and location-tracking features hold it back.

- **Norton Family** makes it easy for parents to track their children's activity across many devices, though it doesn't work on Macs, and its iOS app relies on Apple's free Screen Time feature to do the blocking and tracking.

- **Net Nanny** boasts customizable web filters along with solid screen time and app blocking features, but it's a bit pricey and its geofencing features are not yet competitive.

- **McAfee Safe Family** offers several standard parental control tools and can monitor an unlimited number of PCs and phones. However, its Windows app is sluggish in testing, it does not support macOS devices, and it lacks a web interface.

- You can use parental control software to block access to video streaming apps and sites, as well as limit how much time your child can spend using them.

- Enable Safe-Search. On mobile devices, open your Google app (you may need to download it). Tap on the gear icon, scroll down and tap on Search Settings, and then tap "Filter explicit results" under safesearch filters. On desktops and laptops, go to www.google.com and click Settings in the bottom-right corner; click on Search Settings; and click Turn on safesearch and then Lock safe-search.

- On your kid's phone or tablet. Go to settings. Scroll down and tap screen time. Select content and privacy restrictions and then toggle that feature on.

8 INTERNET SAFETY CHECKLIST

- Keep personal information professional and limited. Tell your kids to never give out their names, email, home address, phone number, account numbers, Social Security number, picture or any other personal information.
- Keep your privacy settings on.
- Practice safe browsing.
- Make sure your internet connection is secure.
- Be careful what you download.
- Choose strong passwords.
- Make online purchases from secure sites.
- Keep your confidential data offline.
- Check a website's reliability.
- Use a strong password. Your online and computer
passwords should be alpha-numeric, at least 8 characters long and include letters (A-Z, mixture of small and capital letters), numbers (0-9) and symbols (#, @, _, &, $). Use different passwords for different accounts, change them regularly
- Use two-factor verification authentication for your accounts.
- Avoid suspicious online and email clickable links.
- Keep your computer updated.
- Beware of free Wi-Fi and downloads.
- Double-check online information.
- Take passwords seriously and very seriously.
- Invest time, money, and effort in enhancing your awareness.
- Always use a VPN while browsing the web. Free VPN may not be the best. Paid is better
- Don't download anything from a website or content provider whom you don't trust.
- Be careful what you post.

- Parents you cannot give what you don't have. Educate yourselves first: Know about online

predators, financial scams, viruses, cyber-bullying and the pervasiveness of pornography on the Internet.

- Talk to your child: Open communication between you and the kid is important in saving and shaping their internet life. Ensure that they can talk to you about things on the Web that make them feel uncomfortable.

- Monitor your children: Be in charge without being possessive. Consider options like sharing an email account, checking your browser's history, clearing cookies, keep the computer in a common room and maintaining access to your kids' accounts.

- Set kids computer or directories to underaged settings: There are a number of search sites geared for children.

- Parental control software: Purchase children version

software that establishes computer user time limits and controls access to sites, games, chat, and file sharing. It can be adapted to offer different levels of control for different ages of children.

- Install protective antivirus: Make sure you have

quality anti-virus, honeypot dummies, anti-spyware, spam blocker and firewall and updated, upgraded security.

- Child friendly devices: Look for digital device

models that are "child-safe," without camera or web-enabled and can limit the numbers the phone can call.

- Shopping online: Check with your parents first and then only buy from trusted online stores.

Watch instant Messaging with caution: If your business uses instant messaging treat it just as you would email and stay on guard from dangerous software.

- Beware of what you share: Ask your parents before you share files and scan your downloaded files for viruses.

ABOUT THE AUTHOR

Dr. Scott Mitnick is a seasoned and experienced Cyber Security expert, a well-respected authority on Internet security. Dr. Mitnick is also a cryptographer, computer security professional, privacy specialist and cybersecurity writer who has worked in service organization as head of cyber security. A man of many parts. His exposure, experience and expertise has endeared him to his colleagues and the internet world. "If it is Dr. Scott Mitnick, they say, it is reliable and trusted cyber security and safety."

Made in the USA
Las Vegas, NV
28 January 2024

85026167R00021